MOVIE · POSTER · BOOK

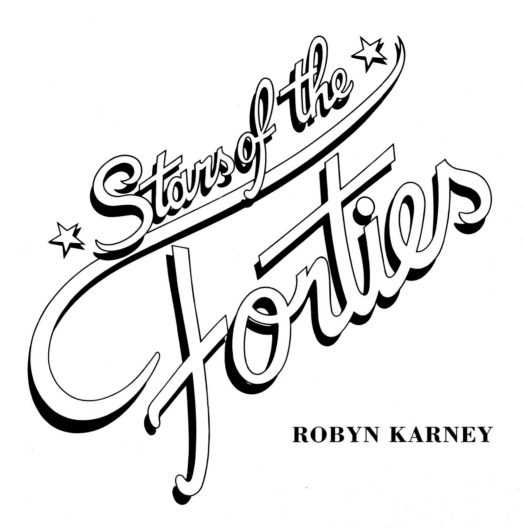

Stars of the
Forties

ROBYN KARNEY

D1362137

OCTOPUS BOOKS

ACKNOWLEDGEMENTS

The publishers thank the following for providing the photographs in this book:
Aquarius Literary Agency, Joel Finler, The Kobal Collection, The Naphthine-Walsh Collection.

First published in 1986 by Octopus Books Limited
59 Grosvenor Street, London W1

© 1986 Octopus Books Limited

ISBN 0 7064 2636 3

First impression

Printed in Hong Kong

CONTENTS

INTRODUCTION

The mid-1930s saw the birth of what is now fondly and respectfully known as The Golden Age of Hollywood. It was a glorious period for the romance of the cinema, and it went on to flourish throughout the 1940s, before falling prey to the considerations of the technological age. For Hollywood that, of course, meant the rising and irreversible challenge of television.

As with the 30s, the 40s was an era of glamour with a capital G and, when we look back with ever-increasing nostalgia on those days when the Dream Factory fed our cherished fantasies so generously, it is, above all, the stars that we remember. Unlike our present day actors and actresses, the stars of yesteryear were more than just skilfully chosen reflections of ourselves — they were larger than life in every sense. The stars of the 40s possessed a unique capacity for portraying suffering; they represented noble ideals and great aspirations, and displayed the virtue of courage in adversity. They were tough, they were daring, but they were also graceful, witty, good-looking and stylish.

The 1940s, moreover, showcased individuality. Certainly, the Hollywood conveyor belt continued to manufacture 'types' for every occasion, but the true stars all had unique qualities to offer. Who could be further removed from dark, bony, aristocratic and glitteringly clever Katharine Hepburn than the almost chubby, pink-cheeked, blonde and 'ordinary' little Betty Grable? What had sultry Lauren Bacall in common with the glowingly healthy swimming athlete, Esther Williams? Suave, sophisticated George Sanders inhabits a different planet from the tough, streetwise John Garfield, and the finely moulded, graceful Cary Grant bore little resemblance to rough-hewn, cynical Humphrey Bogart. But every one of them brought a distinctive personality to the screen, which was somehow skilfully combined with the gift of making us believe in the characters they created.

Of course, not all the stars of the 40s were solely of the period. The handful of great immortals — Hepburn, Barbara Stanwyck, Bette Davis, Gary Cooper, John Wayne — were already famous in the 30s and, indeed, transcended time to endure through the 50s, 60s and, in some cases, the 70s. Others, however (Garfield, for example, and Joan Fontaine), firmly belonged to the decade — a decade of great change for the world, which was reflected in the movies. World War II made patriotism manifest on the screen as never before, and produced a new brand of heroes and heroines. But war also brought the need for relief from its tensions and thus comics such as Bob Hope, and musical stars like Bing Crosby, were tops in popularity. Postwar America saw a new realism in Hollywood, and the tackling of social issues brought stardom to actors of grave demeanour such as Gregory Peck. Conversely, a new, glossy glamour, no better exemplified than by Lana Turner, came into its own.

In this book we bring you a representative selection of pictures (and some interesting words) to remind you of the fabulous stars of this fascinating period.

ALAN LADD

A L A N   L A D D

Born **Hot Springs, Arkansas, 3 September 1913**
Died **1964**

Considering that Alan Ladd died at the age of 50 from a combination of sedatives and alcohol, quite at odds with his image as an action man on screen and a family man off it, it is remarkable that he appeared in 78 films. Ladd was unique in the gallery of big stars of 40s Hollywood. Barely five and a half feet tall (legend has it they stood him on a box to play his love scenes) and, at first glance, somewhat nondescript, he displayed no particular acting talent. Yet, once his opportunity came – as a professional killer in *This Gun For Hire* (1942) – he soon rocketed to become one of the most popular box-office stars of the decade. Blonde, green-eyed, cold and impassive, he seemed tailormade for the *film noir* roles, Westerns and action adventures to which he was assigned. Although always associated with Veronica Lake, the sex symbol with the peek-a-boo hairdo who proved an ideal foil to him, they in fact made only four films together: *This Gun For Hire*, *The Glass Key* (1942), *The Blue Dahlia* (1946) and *Saigon* (1949). As a team, they were a cut-price version of Bogart and Bacall and, indeed, matched the popularity of the more illustrious pair.

Ladd's contract with Paramount came about through the persistent and devoted efforts of his agent, Sue Carol, herself a former film actress who became his second wife in 1942. The studio quickly accustomed itself to the surprise success of their acquisition and began constructing vehicles to suit his image – always the tough guy, and generally teamed with leading ladies of the second division – Donna Reed, Wanda Hendrix, Arlene Dahl – though he graduated between times to Loretta Young (*China*, 1943, *And Now Tomorrow*, 1944), Dorothy Lamour (*Wild Harvest*, 1947), Deborah Kerr (*Thunder In The East*, 1953), Sophia Loren (*Boy On A Dolphin*, 1957). He was immensely popular in Britain, and made a couple of films there, *Hell Below Zero* and *The Black Knight*, ludicrous as a medieval knight in the latter, but nobody seemed to mind. In 1951 Ladd terminated his Paramount contract, eschewing a fortune in the process, because they gave *Detective Story* which he coveted to Kirk Douglas. However, he left them the legacy of George Stevens' high quality Western, *Shane* (1953), the film which has earned him his place in the vintage racks, along with the title role in *The Great Gatsby* (1949).

Alan Ladd was born in Arkansas, raised in California, and was an excellent sportsman at high school. Before becoming a bit player in radio, theatre and the movies, he undertook an inordinate number of jobs including hot dog vendor and, in spite of his stature, lifeguard. Once he left Paramount, the quality of his roles became extremely variable and his last appearance was in *The Carpetbaggers* in 1964, the year of his death. Ladd is surely ripe for revival, especially for those too young to remember him.

with Veronica Lake in *This Gun For Hire*

L A U R E N   B A C A L L

L A U R E N   B A C A L L

Real name **Betty Joan Perske**
Born **New York City, 16 September 1924**

There are few better examples than Lauren Bacall in demonstrating that star quality is not always matched by acting ability. Her most famous film portrayals were notable for her curiously flat and monotonous delivery of lines and a matching facial immobility, largely glacial often sullen. But it was those very qualities, combined with beauty, a powerfully unflinching gaze, and a smouldering, tough sensuality, which added up to what was labelled 'The Look', and which propelled her into stardom. The daughter of divorced parents, she was brought up 'a nice Jewish girl' in New York. Star-struck from an early age (Bette Davis was her film idol), at 16 she spent a year at drama school There followed a couple of years of struggling: fashion-house model, underpaid usherette, a few minor theatre roles. Back to modelling, she made the cover of *Harper's Bazaar*. Mrs Howard Hawks spotted the photo, showed it to her famous director husband and, in the best tradition of Hollywod fiction, he signed her to a seven-year contract (later bought up by Warner Bros.).

The sultry blonde made her debut opposite Humphrey Bogart in *To Have And Have Not* (1944), projecting – under Hawks' expert tutelage – a cool, wisecracking female counterpart to her leading man. Their magic chemistry ignited an otherwise somewhat incoherent movie, and continued to burn off-screen. They were married in 1945,

remaining utterly devoted until Bogie's premature death in 1957 which left Bacall a widow at 31. (She married Jason Robards Jr in 1961; they divorced in 1969). *To Have And Have Not* was followed by *Confidential Agent* (1945), in which she played an unconvincing but provocative English girl opposite Charles Boyer. Three more with her husband – *The Big Sleep* (1946), *Dark Passage* (1947), *Key Largo* (1948) – all traded off her individuality, but she and Warners quarrelled and she suffered several suspensions before buying herself out of her contract and signing with 20th Century-Fox. There came a change of style, notably as one of a trio of golddiggers (with Monroe and Grable) in the musical *How To Marry A Millionaire* (1953).

From the mid-50s Lauren Bacall's screen appearances grew sporadic (*The Gift Of Love*, 1958, *Sex And The Single Girl*, 1965, *Harper*, 1966), but she somehow held on to a place in the public's affections. She made only 22 films in 35 years, and in not one of them was she the lead name. All the more tribute to her unique persona, therefore, that she has made a second career in the theatre, becoming a Broadway star (she won the Tony Award for *Applause*), and finding herself the toast of London's West End in 1985 in Tennessee Williams' play about an ageing actress, *Sweet Bird Of Youth*. Intelligent, witty and warmhearted, this 40s star continues to win converts to her irresistible aura.

with Humphrey Bogart in *To Have and Have Not*

CARY GRANT

C A R Y   G R A N T

Real name **Archibald Alexander Leach**
Born **Bristol, England, 18 January 1904**

For sheer durability in the male glamour stakes, Cary Grant has had no equal. He retired from the screen in 1966, but is still seen at public functions sporting a head of white hair and, given his age of 81, as handsome as ever. Sophisticated, witty, urbane, boyish, debonair – all are adjectives which spring to mind in attempting to describe his timeless qualities. But, above all, was the devastating aura of charm that characterised his screen persona.

His origins belie his image somewhat. He ran away from a broken home, joined a troupe of travelling knockabout comics in vaudeville, became expert at acrobatics and mime, and was chosen for a tour of the US in 1920. He stayed on in New York, finally heading West in 1931, and was contracted for five years by Paramount, who cast him in a rag-bag of supporting roles until he was promoted to *Blonde Venus* (1932) with Marlene Dietrich, and then cast as Mae West's romantic lead in *She Done Him Wrong* and *I'm No Angel* (both 1933). Grant first co-starred with Katharine Hepburn in the disastrous *Sylvia Scarlett* (1936) and shared the honours with Irene Dunne in *The Awful Truth* (1937). Then it was back with Miss Hepburn for two huge hits, Howard Hawks' *Bringing Up Baby*, and *Holiday*, directed by George Cukor (both 1938). The age of the screwball comedy had arrived and so, very definitely, had Cary Grant. The 40s saw him in a string of now classic successes, including *Suspicion* (1941) with Joan Fontaine, the first of four for Hitchcock, *Notorious* (1946) opposite Ingrid Bergman, and the hilarious *I Was A Male War Bride* with Ann Sheridan. In fact, his roster of leading ladies reads like a list of Hollywood's most attractive women: Loretta Young, Myrna Loy, Rosalind Russell, Deborah Kerr, Sophia Loren, Grace Kelly, Eve Marie Saint.

In real life, too, Grant – sartorially impeccable and with a highly individual speaking voice (brilliantly parodied by Tony Curtis in *Some Like It Hot*) – seems irresistible to women. He has had five wives in as many decades, the first being actress Virginia Cherrill, the second the famed Woolworth heiress Barbara Hutton. His position as Hollywood's foremost romantic lead even survived unscathed a scandalous divorce from Dyan Cannon – wife number four and the mother of his only child, a daughter, born when he was past 60 – as well as a reputation for meanness of the 'last to pay for the drinks' variety. He picked up a couple of Oscar nominations but never won, perhaps because the stylish, largely comedy roles in which he excelled were considered too lightweight for the ultimate accolade. All his co-stars however, testify to the discipline, concentration and hard work that went into the seemingly effortless result and, at the 1970 Oscar ceremonies, he received a special award for his contribution to the American cinema.

with Ann Sheridan in I Was A Male War Bride

R I T A   H A Y W O R T H

RITA HAYWORTH

Real name **Margarita Carmen Cansino**
Born **Brooklyn, New York, 17 October 1918**

The most enduring image of Rita Hayworth is as *Gilda* (1946), showing her in the clinging black dress and elbow length gloves in which she sang (dubbed) 'Put The Blame On Mame', a provocative hymn to eroticism which inflamed the male cinema-going world. The movie was the highlight of a career which began when, as a teenager, she was seen dancing in a Mexican club by Fox production head Winfield Sheehan and signed up, making her debut as an unnoticed dancer in *Under The Pampas Moon* (1935).

When Fox merged with 20th Century she was dropped and, in 1937, aged 19, married Edward Judson, a business-man over 20 years her senior. He changed her name to Hayworth, made over her raven hair into a cascade of auburn tresses, and got her a contract with Columbia. A clutch of forgotten Bs preceded her first good role in *Only Angels Have Wings* (1941). More Bs followed, and a series of loanouts which led her to sparkle opposite James Cagney in *The Strawberry Blonde* (1941). At last Rita, already a popular pin-up, was given her due and grabbed by 20th Century-Fox to play a temptress, ravishing in Technicolor, opposite Tyrone power in *Blood And Sand*. Now one of Hollywood's most potent Love Goddesses, she was given some excellent vehicles at Columbia, including *You'll Never Get Rich* (1941) and *You Were Never Lovelier* (1942), two films in which she made an alluring dancing partner for

Fred Astaire. For Fox again, she was a delight in *My Gal Sal* (1942), falling in love with co-star, Victor Mature, and divorcing Judson. It was not the hunky Victor she married, but the chunky Orson Welles who later cropped his wife's hair and dyed it blonde for *The Lady From Shanghai* (1948), a thriller in which Welles' evident infatuation with Rita belied the fact that their marriage was over.

The Lady From Shanghai was Hayworth's last film of any note. She was saddled with poor vehicles, her box-office appeal diminished and, in 1948, to the chagrin of Columbia's boss, Harry Cohn, she eloped with millionaire playboy, Prince Aly Khan. They married in 1949 and had a daughter but two years later she was back, divorced and broke, and pleading with Cohn for reinstatement. She staggered on through the 50s, embarking on another disastrous two-year marriage to Dick Haymes. *Separate Tables* (1958) brought her a better role and a marriage (duration three years) to producer James Hill, but by the mid-70s, she had fallen victim to severe alcoholism. Worse came with Alzheimer's disease, a vicious form of creeping senility, and, in 1981, she was consigned to the custody of her daughter. Such was the fate of the fabled beauty who commanded a quarter of a million dollars at her peak, and whose pin-up adorned the atomic bomb which was dropped at Bikini. A cruelly prophetic accolade.

in *Gilda*

H U M P H R E Y   B O G A R T

H U M P H R E Y   B O G A R T

Born New York City, 25 December 1899
Died 1957

The voice was nasal and gravelly; the eyes – always on the edge of bloodshot – conveyed a mixture of exhausted cynicism and alert understanding; the lived-in face was characterised by a vulpine mouth (caused by a war injury to his lip which resulted in his lisp). Humphrey Bogart, in short, was very different from the popular image of a romantic idol but, having attained that status in the 40s, he has remained the most popular of them all, worshipped by a generation of fans not yet born in his heyday.

The son of a middle-class New York surgeon, Bogart experienced a comfortable but emotionally cold and tense upbringing. He flunked out of college and joined the US Navy during World War I, more as an act of escape than of patriotism. He returned to a New York in the grip of Jazz Age fever and took advantage of its pleasures, drifting into the theatre for want of interest in anything more solid, and played a succession of supporting roles, often callow juveniles. It took 14 years of slog around Broadway before the break came. He was cast as gangster Duke Mantee in Robert Sherwood's 'The Petrified Forest', with Leslie Howard in the lead, and made an impact. Howard insisted that Warner Bros. use Bogart for the film version, and a new screen gangster-cum-anti-hero emerged in 1936. He made 28 movies in the next four years, including *Dead End (1937)*, *The Amazing Dr Clitterhouse* (1938), and *They*

Drive By Night (1940), but stardom came with *High Sierra* (1941). It was very successful, and marked the beginning of Bogart's collaboration with John Huston who had co-written it. They made several together with Huston directing, starting with *The Maltese Falcon* (1941) which took Bogart to super-stardom, and including *the African Queen* (1952) which gave the star his last great role and an Oscar. It was the Huston films, plus two Hawks classics (*To Have And Have Not*, 1944, *The Big Sleep*, 1946) and, of course, the deathless favourite, *Casablanca* (1942), which today constitute the focus of the Bogart legend.

In private life Bogey was on his third marriage when he fell in love with his co-star on *To Have And Have Not*. Lauren Bacall, many years his junior, became his fourth wife, gave him two children and brought him great happiness until his premature death from throat cancer in 1957. Hard-drinking, hard-living, and possessed of a gallows humour, he faced illness and death with exemplary courage. Alistair Cooke published an eloquent obituary in which he commented that Bogart was '. . . a man with a tough shell and a fine core . . . By showily neglecting his outward forms of grace he kept inferior men at a distance . . . From all of them he was determined to keep his secret – the rather shameful one in the realistic world we inhabit, of being a gallant man and an idealist'.

in *The Big Sleep*

K A T H A R I N E   H E P B U R N

KATHARINE HEPBURN

Born **Hartford, Connecticut, 9 November 1907**

Aristocratic in bearing, strong willed, and fiercely protective of her privacy (she still refuses to comment on her relationship with Spencer Tracy), Katharine Hepburn became a star with her screen debut opposite John Barrymore in *A Bill Of Divorcement* (1932). The daughter of a cultivated New England family – mother a suffragette, father a distinguished surgeon – she grew up in an atmosphere of spiritual freedom, intellectual rigour and physical discipline. She built a Broadway career before arriving in Hollywood, bringing a fresh wind of intelligence and independence with her.

Contracted by RKO, she delivered a string of hits – *Morning Glory*, *Little Women* (both 1933), *The Little Minister* (1934), *Alice Adams* (1935) – picking up the first of her four Oscars and two of her eleven nominations. However, with her feminist views, she was sympathetic to such roles as the lady flyer in *Christopher Strong* (1933) and the girl disguised as a boy in *Sylvia Scarlett* (1935). Both were flops, as were *Mary Of Scotland* and *A Woman Rebels* (both 1936) and, despite enjoying huge success with Cary Grant in *Bringing Up Baby* and *Holiday* in 1938, Hepburn was labelled box-office poison and departed for Broadway. She starred in Philip Barry's smash hit, 'The Philadelphia Story', and had the foresight to buy the film rights. Thus, in 1940, she returned to Hollywood in triumph to make the movie, picking up another Oscar nomination and embarking on a second winning streak which has lasted to this day, but which peaked in the 40s.

It was during 1941 that the Tracy-Hepburn association began. Their personal devotion became an open secret, conducted with discretion (Tracy, a devout Catholic, was married) and, unusually, was treated with respect by the movie colony. Their nine films together showed them as sparring partners rather than romantic figures, upending tradition in making the woman the stronger character and even, in *Woman Of The Year* (1941), the heel of the pair. Another superb example was *Adam's Rib* (1949), in which they played married lawyers on opposite sides of a case.

In the 50s, Hepburn's liberated heroines were replaced by a series of moving middle-aged spinsters, most memorably with Humphrey Bogart in *The African Queen* (1951), and as the schoolteacher in *Summertime* (1955), finding first-time but short lived romance in Venice with Rossano Brazzi. In the 60s she was masterly as the drug-addicted mother in *Long Day's Journey Into Night* then, in 1967, was reunited with a dying Spencer Tracy in *Guess Who's Coming To Dinner?*, winning another Oscar. *On Golden Pond* (1981), with a dying Henry Fonda, brought her fourth Oscar and a sad echo of her immortal relationship with Tracy. She now lives alone in retirement.

with Judy Holliday in *Adam's Rib*

ROBERT MITCHUM

ROBERT MITCHUM

Born Bridgeport, Connecticut, 6 August 1917

Robert Mitchum has appealed to four generations of cinemagoers while lazily, relaxedly and laconically portraying tough guys, soldiers, nice young men, *film noir* villains, psychopaths, cowboys, detectives, and urban man. With his distinctive good looks – the eyes sleepy and inscrutable, the set of the cleft chin – and effortless delivery, Mitchum's secret is that he has always been essentially himself, belonging to no man, no time, no place. His personality settles easily into any mould, making him equally effective as John Wayne's buddy in the comedy Western *El Dorado* (1967), or as Sarah Miles' husband in the romantic *Ryan's Daughter* (1970).

Mitchum started as an extra in 1943. Before that he spent several years in rough jobs such as ditch-digging, before going to work in the Lockheed aircraft factory. Married in 1940 (the Mitchums are one of Hollywood's longest running couples), he was looking to earn money, and took movie work where he could get it. He appeared as a bit player in 16 movies in 1943 alone, before being noticed in *Cry Havoc* for MGM, who re-engaged him for a small part in *30 Seconds Over Tokyo* (1944). He was chalking up what would be a record number of war films, and was contracted by RKO, who loaned him to UA for what proved to be his first substantial role, the tough, world-weary officer in *The Story Of GI Joe* (1945). It won him a

Best Supporting Actor nomination, his one and only brush with the Oscar. For the sad aspect of Mitchum's career is that he has been repeatedly wasted in inferior material and, while he is one of the highest paid stars, few people are able to pinpoint his successes. One of them, though, was as the murderous preacher in *The Night Of The Hunter* (1955), actor Charles Laughton's distinguished directorial effort, in which Mitchum was cast because Laughton considered him 'one of the best actors in the world'.

The actor's lazy persona belies a skilled professional who works extraordinarily hard and commands the widespread respect of his colleagues. He was dogged for some years by his reputation as a lawless hellraiser, fuelled by being jailed on a marijuana charge. The verdict was later set aside and the charge held to be trumped up. In truth he is gentle, humorous and considerate. Deborah Kerr, who co-starred with him in *The Sundowners* (1960) and *Heaven Knows Mr Allison* (1957), records that he was one of her two favourite leading men (David Niven was the other). Mitchum's first notable lead was as the revenge-seeking cowboy in the splendid, brooding Western, *Pursued* (1947). Thirty years on, only the greying of the hair betrayed that he had changed at all as he continued to star in the sort of movies (for example, the remake of *Farewell My Lovely*, 1974) in which he might so easily have starred in the 40s.

with Deborah Kerr in Heaven Knows Mr Allison

ABBOTT & COSTELLO

ABBOTT & COSTELLO

Real names William A. Abbott; Louis Francis Cristillo
Born Asbury Park, NJ, 2 October 1895; Paterson, NJ, 6 March 1906
Died 1974; 1959

No survey of stars of the 40s would be representative without Bud Abbott and Lou Costello, the comedy team who featured in the Top Ten stars list from 1941-45 and from 1948-51, and whose films were among the top ten box-office grosses for the entire decade. Lou Costello, the roly-poly fat man, was the comic while tall, thin, poker-faced Bud Abbott was the straight man. Lou was a salesman before trying his hand as a prizefighter in an effort to save money to get to Hollywood. Once there he had to content himself with a job as a labourer on the MGM lot, but later became a stunt man, on one occasion doubling for the glamorous Dolores Del Rio, before moving into vaude-ville. During a Brooklyn engagement, his ailing straight man was unable to appear and the theatre's box-office clerk stepped in. He was Bud Abbott, the son of circus folk, who had had a colourful youth at sea, since when he had been trying unsuccessfully to break into show business.

Thus, the partnership was born and, after several years on the burlesque circuit, they landed a spot on Kate Smith's radio show which led to an appearance in a 1939 Broadway Revue. Universal picked them up for supporting roles in a musical, *One Night In The Tropics* (1940), then signed them to a long-term contract, starring them in *Buck Privates* (1941) with The Andrews Sisters. The movie grossed $10 million and the studio hastily repeated the formula with *In The Navy* and *Keep 'Em Flying* that same year. Endless variations were found, enabling the boys to exploit their particular line of verbal crossfire, conducted amidst slapstick and propped up by conventional stars and subsidiary romantic plots. Their routines derived from burlesque and, inevitably, began to run out of steam as the decade progressed. Their flagging popularity was revived with *Abbott And Costello Meet Frankenstein* (1948) with Lon Chaney, Bela Lugosi and Glen Strange, thus providing a new recipe in which they met *The Killer Boris Karloff* and *The Invisible Man*, not to mention *Captain Kidd* (Charles Laughton), and *The Keystone Kops*. By the mid-50s, their appeal was dead. Abbott retired, Costello went it alone in *The Thirty-Foot Bride Of Candy Rock* (1959), a barely released disaster, after which he died of a heart attack. Abbott, broke and ill and hounded by the Internal Revenue, lingered on until 1974, suffering a series of strokes and finally dying of cancer.

Looking back on the duo, it is almost impossible to account for their success. Unlike their illustrious predecessors, Laurel and Hardy, they were not very clever or appealing. They failed to find favour with critics, and have no following among present day TV viewers. One must conclude that they hit a freak mood at large in the American public which was lost forever by the 50s.

with Patricia Medina in *Abbot And Costello In The Foreign Legion*

BETTE DAVIS

B E T T E   D A V I S

Real name **Ruth Elizabeth Davis**
Born **Lowell, Massachusetts, 5 April 1908**

A popular movie buff's game is to list a series of brief synopses from which to identify a film. Here, with answers supplied, are some examples: she deceives her cellist husband about her former lover then murders the latter (*Deception*, 1946); guilty of a hit-and-run- killing, she pins it on the negro cook's son (*In This Our Life*, 1942); she persuades the pregnant Mary Astor to conceal her condition, and give her the baby to pass off as her own (*The Great Lie*, 1941); she makes a public mockery of her lover at a ball but fights through plague-infested swamps to go to him when he is taken ill (*Jezebel*, 1938). A tiny sample of the material that Bette Davis, undisputed First Lady of the American Sceen, made her own, elevating even the most ludicrous hokum into art and enslaving millions of adoring fans who were by turns shocked, enthralled, delighted, and moved to genuine tears by her outrageous antics.

No actress has been more impersonated or parodied, for her passionate and intelligent portrayals were framed by a highly individual set of physical mannerisms – the clipped New England tones, the flouncing walk, the nervous stabbing way with her inseparable prop, a cigarette. The recipient of 10 Academy nominations, two Oscars, and the first American Film Institute Life Achievement Award to be given to a woman, it all began with supporting roles in 1931. She had 22 films behind her when she electrified the cinema as the amoral waitress who destroys a medical student (Leslie Howard) in *Of Human Bondage* (1934). Her incomparable gallery of neurasthenics, including the frustrated spinster in *Now Voyager* (1942), was ably complemented by reliable women as in *Watch On The Rhine* (1943), comedies such as *June Bride* (1948) and tragic heroines as in her famed *Dark Victory* (1939). But the two most celebrated monuments to her talents are undoubtedly the ruthless Regina in *The Little Foxes* (1942), and her last great role in what was, happily, a superb screenplay, that of Margo Channing, a famous Broadway star fighting the onset of age in *All About Eve* (1950). Her standing took a nosedive in the 50s, driving her to advertise her services in 'Variety', but she came back fighting, between some appalling films, to renewed fame during the 60s with two baroque horror offerings, *Whatever Happened To Baby Jane?* and *Hush, Hush, Sweet Charlotte*. Old, but very definitely vintage, she was striking in *Death On The Nile* (1978) and is still going strong, starring in superior made-for-TV movies.

Her approach to her work, her fierce independence and integrity, her marriages, and her notorious court battle with Warner Bros., are all wonderfully chronicled in her autobiography, 'The Lonely Life', in which she writes, 'I suppose I'm larger than life. That's my problem. Created in a fury, I'm at home in a tempest'.

with Trevor Howard in *The Petrified Forest*

JOHN WAYNE

JOHN WAYNE

Real name **Marion Michael Morrison**
Born **Winterset, Iowa, 26 May 1907**
Died **1979**

Widely known as Duke, John Wayne grew up in California and went to USC on a football scholarship. In 1928, he became a tough bit-part player then, in 1930, he was given his first Western lead in *The Big Trail* and, in the following eight years, notched up a further 80 films, mostly lowly boots-and-saddle B's. His last Western was *The Shootist* in 1976, three years before his death after a long and very courageous battle with cancer. In the 40-odd years between, he made an almost countless number of movies which, although they included some war films such as *Sands Of Iwo Jima* (1949) which earned him his first Oscar nomination, adventure stories, and the Irish romance, *The Quiet Man* (1952), largely followed the Western trail.

Indissolubly linked with director John Ford in public memory, it was actually Howard Hawks who helped Wayne to realise his full potential as an interpreter of complex, independent-minded loners in the great classic Western *Red River* (1948). His portrayal of a rancher determined to get his huge herd to market against overwhelming odds of distance, difficult terrain and the Indian threat, while locked in conflict with his adopted son (Montgomery Clift), catapulted Wayne to super-stardom. It was after this that Ford passed the much quoted remark, 'I didn't know that big son of a bitch could act' – although he had given the actor his first notable lead as The Ringo Kid in *Stagecoach*

(1938), and used him again in *The Long Voyage Home* (1940) and *They Were Expendable* (1945). Director and star teamed up for the remake of *Three Godfathers* (1948), followed by the famous, so-called cavalry trilogy – *Fort Apache* (1948), *She Wore A Yellow Ribbon* (1949), and *Rio Grande* (1950). Ford also directed Wayne in *The Quiet Man* (1952), and in the superlative revenge Western, *The Searchers* (1956). By the late 40s, Wayne was already an independent producer-star, but nothing of note originated from his stable, and his only directing venture, *The Alamo* (1960), was a turgid expression of pioneering patriotism. For the Duke made no secret of his arch-conservative politics, and two of his own productions, the shamelessly Red-scare *Big Jim McLain* (1952) and the pro-Vietnam *The Green Berets* (1968), betrayed his macho represent-ation of the moral majority in no uncertain terms. None of this, however, seemed to hamper his continuing charis-matic image as the archetypal American hero, who also displayed a comedy touch in two Hawks films, *Rio Bravo* (1959) and its hilarious follow-up, *El Dorado* (1967).

Thrice married and father of seven children, John Wayne finally won an Oscar for *True Grit* (1969) at the age of 62. By the time of his death, he had assumed the status of an American legend, and had gained the rare distinction of having a Congressional Medal struck in his honour.

with Barry Fitzgerald in *The Quiet Man*

JOAN FONTAINE

JOAN FONTAINE

Real name Joan de Beauvoir de Havilland
Born Tokyo, Japan, 22 October 1917

Joan Fontaine is a woman of many accomplishments. Not only is she a Cordon Bleu cook, an expert golfer and an interior decorator, but also a licensed pilot, a ballooning champion and a prizewinning tuna fisherman. She was born of British parents who later divorced, and grew up in the US. She entered the movies in the 30s, in the shadow of her already successful sister, Olivia de Havilland. Her film engagements, initially as Joan Burfield, led nowhere, in spite of being cast opposite Fred Astaire in *A Damsel In Distress* (1937). Her serene prettiness, which would mature into elegant and sophisticated blonde beauty, was an advantage to her small role as Douglas Fairbanks Jr's love interest in *Gunga Din* (1939), and her appealing vulnerability enhanced her sympathetic, but again small, role in George Cukor's famous screen version of *The Women* (1939). By the end of the 30s, however, she didn't seem to be making much progress. RKO had dropped her contract, she was about to marry actor Brian Aherne (the first of her four husbands), and had virtually decided to give up acting.

It was at this point that she found herself seated at dinner next to David Selznick, who was looking to cast the gauche, sensitive, mousy heroine of Daphne du Maurier's best-selling novel, 'Rebecca', and decided he might have found her in his dinner companion. A test proved him correct, and Joan was launched. Co-starred with Laurence Olivier and directed by Alfred Hitchcock, she won an Oscar nomination and a substantial public following, as demonstrated by the readers of 'Picturegoer', who voted her their Gold Medal. Also for Hitchcock, her next film was *Suspicion* (1941); paired with a dazzlingly debonair Cary Grant, she was again a somewhat naive wife, and this time she won the coveted Oscar. Heroines radiating an air of innocence continued to come her way, including *Jane Eyre* (1944) with Orson Welles, and *The Constant Nymph* (1945) for which she was again Oscar nominated. But the 40s was a rich period for romantic melodrama and *film noir* and she got her opportunities in both, even managing an Edwardian lady poisoner in *Ivy* (1947).

The zenith of Joan Fontaine's career was *Letter From An Unknown Woman* (1948), directed by Max Ophuls and co-starring Louis Jourdan. Set in *fin-de-siècle* Vienna, it was a tragic account of a woman who sacrifices her life to her love for an attractive but utterly irresponsible concert pianist. A good story, well-filmed, it allowed the star to display grace, sophistication and dignity, combined with warmth, sensuality and a haunting echo of her own early vulnerability. Alas, the ingredients which had resulted in this wistful period romance, did not come Fontaine's way again and, although she contined working into the 60s, the 40s will always be remembered as her Golden Age.

in Jane Eyre

B A R B A R A   S T A N W Y C K

BARBARA STANWYCK

Real name **Ruby Stevens**
Born **Brooklyn, New York, 16 July 1907**

The wisdom of hindsight now acknowledges Barbara Stan-wyck as one of the handful of all-time Hollywood Greats and in 1981 the Academy went some way to atoning for its disgrace in never having given her the coveted award by presenting her with a special honorary Oscar – which she accepted with the charm and dignity befitting a true star. She did, however, collect four Best Actress nominations in the course of her varied and distinguished career, and the roles which earned them are an eloquent testimony to her versatility: *Stella Dallas* (1937), in which she suffered and emoted as the vulgar but well-intentioned mother of a daughter whose social status she is determined to raise; *Ball Of Fire* (1942), one of the great screwball comedies of the period, in which she was sexy, touching and hilarious as a moll inadvertently caught up with a bunch of absent-minded professors led by Gary Cooper; *Double Indemnity* (1944), Billy Wilder's definitive, classic *film noir* which gave her her best-known role as a brassy, sullen, gold-digging murderess; *Sorry, Wrong Number* (1948) as the helplessly bedridden invalid menaced by the theat of murder.

Stanwyck's background was exceedingly humble. Orphaned early on, she lived with her sister and quit school at 13, supporting herself with a series of menial jobs while training as a dancer, and finally broke into the theatre in New York. Her first marriage (her second and last was to Robert Taylor from 1939-52) took her to Hollywood and a couple of bit parts in the last years of the silents. She first made a real impression as the vulnerable young girl caught up with a Chinese warlord in *The Bitter Tea Of General Yen* (1933), but it was *Stella Dallas* which elevated her to stardom and trail-blazed her extraordinary winning streak in the 40s, outclassing Joan Crawford for melodrama with *The Strange Love Of Martha Ivers* (1946), and rivalling Jean Arthur for charm as a con woman opposite Henry Fonda in *The Lady Eve* (1941). In the 50s, Stanwyck's special brand of toughness found new expression with the revival of the Western, and she held her own as the *Cattle Queen Of Montana* (1954) with Ronald Reagan, in *The Violent Men* (1955) with Edward G. Robinson and as the lady rancher in *40 Guns* (1957). The 60s saw the decline and end of her movie career, but she distinguished herself on TV, winning an Emmy Award, and in the 80s returned to the small screen to appear in *The Thorn Birds*.

In 1944, Barbara Stanwyck was declared the highest paid woman in America. She now lives in semi-retirement, revered by her colleagues who share the sentiments of Cecil B. DeMille. He directed her but once, in *Union Pacific* (1939), classed her his favourite actress, and recorded 'I have never worked with an actress who was more co-operative, less temperamental, and a better workman'.

with Kirk Douglas in *The Strange Love of Martha Ivers*

BING CROSBY

BING CROSBY

Real name **Harry Lillis Crosby**
Born **Tacoma, Washington, 2 May 1901**
Died **1977**

In 1944, Paramount released a gentle, slightly sentimental, comedy-drama about a young priest taking over a New York parish from its aging incumbent and proceeding to charm everyone he encounters. The film was Leo McCarey's *Going My Way*, which grossed an astronomical fortune and won six Oscars, including Best Picture, and Best Actor for the priest. He was Bing Crosby who, in real-life too, had been charming all comers since he was a college boy musician.

Bing was barely out of his teens when he started touring the country with his college friend, Al Rinker, who was gifted in arranging popular songs of the day in a style that was fresh and new, and that suited Bing's relaxed, individualistic and lilting vocal quality. They were later joined by Harry Barris, and enjoyed much success as The Rhythm Boys, playing vaudeville and nightclub circuits and becoming well-known radio performers. Their big break came when they were invited to join Paul Whiteman's band, and it was as a Whiteman singer that Crosby got to Hollywood to perform in *King Of Jazz* (1930). Paramount signed him to a contract the following year, and he crooned his way effortlessly through the 30s in a series of amiable musicals such as *College Humor* (1933), *Anything Goes* (1936) and *Dr Rhythm* (1938). His records sold by the millions, and no disc has ever topped the sales – over 25 million – of his version of 'White Christmas' which he first sang in *Holiday Inn* (1941). It was during the 40s that Crosby progressed to super-stardom. There were a few good musicals (*Birth Of The Blues*, 1941, *Dixie*, 1943, *Blue Skies*, 1946); there was *Going My Way* and its even more successful sequel, *The Bells Of St Mary's* (1945) opposite Ingrid Bergman. Above all, there were the phenomenally successful *Road* films which teamed Bing with his friend, Bob Hope, and Dorothy Lamour. Crosby's film career slowly declined in the 50s and 60s, though *The Country Girl* (1954), for which he was Oscar-nominated, and *High Society* (1956) – both with Grace Kelly – remain memorable.

Bing Crosby died of a heart attack during a game of golf when he was 73. Since his death, a few books and TV documentaries have set out to dispel the illusion that he was Mr Nice Guy. His first wife, Dixie Lee, who had a miserably lonely life and suffered from alcoholism, and his four sons, apparently took second place to his beloved golf course, and the occasional barroom binge was known to interfere with his commitments. Dixie died of cancer in 1952, and Crosby, the second richest man in show business after Bob Hope, married Kathryn Grant, 30 years his junior, in 1957, and raised a second family of three children. Whatever the truth of otherwise or his shortcomings, he remains in the records as one of the best-loved entertainers of all time.

with Bob Hope in *Road to Singapore*

JUDY GARLAND

J U D Y   G A R L A N D

Real name **Frances Gumm**
Born **Grand Rapids, Minnesota, 10 June 1922**
Died **1969**

An experienced performer from the age of three, she was contracted to MGM in 1936. Three years later, aged 16, she was cast as Dorothy in *The Wizard Of Oz* and found herself on the yellow brick road to stardom. It was not long before fame began to exact its price. A studio doctor prescribed pills for overweight which, combined with overwork, took a toll on her nerves and initiated a lifelong cycle of pill-taking – for sleeping, for waking up, for calming down, to suppress her appetite. By the time of her tragic death, aged 47, she had had five husbands, numerous nervous breakdowns, several suicide attempts, studio suspensions, lawsuits, and a notorious reputation for unreliability.

The rise and fall of Judy Garland has been chronicled in gory detail in innumerable books, serving perhaps to obscure the most important fact about her: she was a performer of the first magnitude on stage and screen, who possessed a unique combination of gifts and brought untold pleasure to countless millions. The extravagance of serious critics' praise almost defies belief, indicating the lengths to which people would go in an effort to define the nature of Garland's unique artistry and appeal. She combined passion, stridency, humour and warmth with a vulnerability that was powerfully moving, and the package was wrapped with a nervous edge that betrayed her tremulous hold on herself but which brought magic to her screen persona. The youthful version of these qualities was seen in several films with Mickey Rooney, notably *Babes In Arms*, *Strike Up The Band* (both 1940) and *Babes On Broadway* (1941) – all firmly establishing her as a rising star.

Judy blossomed into a new radiance in *Meet Me In St Louis* (1944). It was directed by Vincente Minnelli, who became her second husband and father of their daughter Liza. Throughout the decade, although increasingly dogged by personal problems, she appeared in a crop of excellent musicals, among them *The Pirate* (1947) with Gene Kelly and *Easter Parade* (1948) with Fred Astaire. There was straight drama too: a poignant wartime romance, *The Clock*, with Robert Walker in 1945 and, much later, *Judgement At Nuremberg* (1961) and *A Child Is Waiting* (1963). Sadly, her last film, *I Could Go On Singing* (1963), was a poor vehicle in which she gave an edgy portrayal of herself – bloated, nervous, tired, but still moving. Her testament, however, is *A Star Is Born* (1954), produced by her then husband, Sid Luft, co-starring James Mason, directed by George Cukor, and representing her comeback after a long rough patch. As a small-time singer who rises to stardom and pays for it with personal tragedy, Garland gave a virtuoso performance which displayed all her gifts to the full. That she failed to win the Oscar remains, as one commentator put it, 'the film city's greatest injustice'.

with Ray Bolger in *The Wizard of Oz*

GREGORY PECK

GREGORY PECK

Real name **Eldred Gregory Peck**
Born **La Jolla, California, 5 April 1916**

Generally considered the nicest man in Hollywood and – as is so often the irony of life – one of the most boring, Gregory Peck, not surprisingly, became a star playing nice guys. Hallmarked by a personality that spells earnest sincerity and serious virtue, his dependable, sometimes crusading, heroes also had the advantage of his tall, dark and handsome looks, thoroughly masculine but with an appealing air of sensitivity and an attractively velvety voice.

Peck studied at San Diego University but became interested in acting, joined New York's Neighborhood Playhouse, and then enjoyed a successful Broadway debut in 'Morning Star' by Emlyn Williams. Turned down by the army due to an injury incurred at college, he was available to Hollywood when many of the leading men were still at war. It was scriptwriter-producer Casey Robinson who first used him in *Days Of Glory* (1944), a wartime propaganda piece which came and went, but in which Peck made a huge impression and had the major studios competing for his services. But he was the first of his contemporaries to assert independence, refusing long-term contracts, having a say in his material, and becoming ever richer. His second role, as the priest in *The Keys Of The Kingdom* (1945), won his first Oscar nomination and secured his star position. That same year he went from strength to strength, starring with Greer Garson as a millionaire who marries a servant girl in *The Valley Of Decision*, and then playing an amnesiac opposite Ingrid Bergman in Hitchcock's *Spellbound*. He was Oscar-nominated for *The Yearling* (1946), and for *Gentleman's Agreement* (1947), the year's Best Picture in which he was ideally cast as an investigative journalist exposing the evils of anti-semitism by posing as a Jew. He wasn't too successful as a lecher in *Duel In The Sun* (1947), nor too convincing as an English barrister in *The Paradine Case* (1948), but won a fourth nomination for *Twelve O'Clock High* (1950), in command of a bombing mission. He was splendid in the Western, *The Gunfighter* (1950), after which his career slipped into periods of decline, not to say disaster (notably *Beloved Infidel*, 1959, a hysterical and inept piece about Scott Fitzgerald and Sheilah Graham), punctuated by some modest and pleasing ventures, and a few big-time till-ringers such as *The Snows Of Kilimanjaro* (1952), with Ava Gardner, *The Guns Of Navarone* (1961), and *To Kill A Mockingbird* (1962) for which he finally won his Oscar. Most recently, he was in *The Boys From Brazil* (1978) and *The Sea Wolves* (1980).

Gregory Peck is still, at the age of 70, a tireless worker for good causes, a past president of the American Film Institute and of the Academy, has written an autobiography, 'An Actor's Life', and is a recipient of the Jean Hersholt Humanitarian Award.

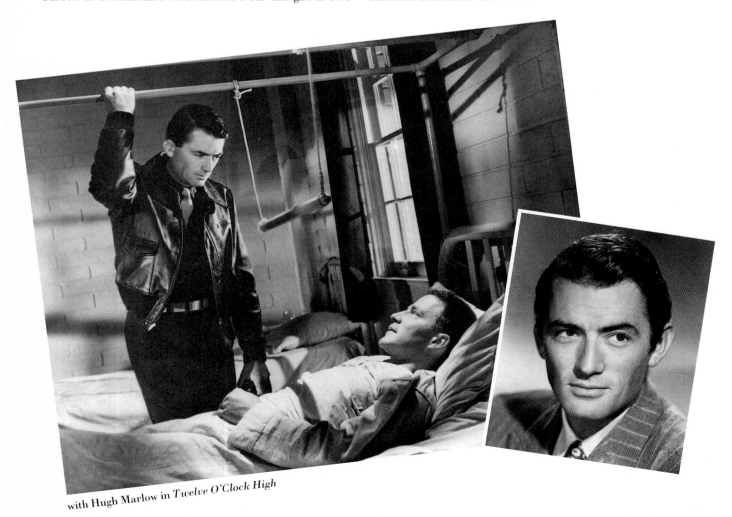

with Hugh Marlow in *Twelve O'Clock High*

B O B   H O P E

BOB HOPE

Real name **Leslie Hope**
Born **Eltham, England, 29 May 1903**

Among the best songs composed by Ralph Rainger and Leo Robin is one called 'Thanks For The Memory'. Haunting, nostalgic and romantically witty, it won an Oscar with its first airing in *The Big Broadcast Of 1938*, and became the well-known signature tune of the man who sang it. He, of course, was Bob Hope, as unlikely a purveyor for such sentiment as ever there was. Hope grew up in the US, acquiring a persona as American as the ice-cream soda he once dispensed during a series of menial jobs. It was in vaudeville that he developed his stand-up comic routines which took him to New York and, in 1933, to a role in the hit musical, 'Roberta'. But it was his popularity on radio that really made a mark and took him to Hollywood.

In spite of his plain looks – over-accentuated features, a head that appears too big for his stocky body – nondescript singing voice, and an absence of true actor's ability, he became a major movie attraction of the 40s. Relying largely on a line in rapid-fire verbal patter (to which end he employed the largest army of gag-writers ever in the service of one man), Hope, it must be said, is an acquired taste. Enough people, however, relished the flavour to ensure him a place in the top ten studio moneymakers for a dozen or so years. Paramount was the lucky recipient, and it all got under way with the comedy thriller, *The Cat And The Canary* (1939), a big success that suited his personality. But

it was the *Road* films that turned this one-note entertainer into a movie star. In 1940, he was teamed with Bing Crosby and Dorothy Lamour in a lightweight romantic comedy, *Road To Singapore*. The film grossed a fortune far beyond its expectations, leading to five progressively zanier sequels. *Zanzibar* (1941) followed, then came *Morocco* (1942), *Utopia* (1945), *Rio* (1947) and, in Technicolor, *Bali* (1952), the last and least, with the formula and the stars visibly flagging. (*Road To Hong Kong* ten years later was a feeble British-made attempt to revive the past, with Joan Collins replacing Lamour.) In between times and, indeed, for another 30-odd years, Hope made an impressive number of other movies. The best and most successful was *The Paleface* (1948) while among other remembered efforts were *Monsieur Beaucaire* (1945), *Sorrowful Jones* (1949) and *The Lemon Drop Kid* (1951).

In private life, he is estimated as the wealthiest man in show biz, reputedly worth between $400 and $700 million in big business interests. He has one of the happiest marriages in Hollywood (since 1934 to Dolores Reade), is a devotee of the golf course and plays for charity, an inveterate emcee of Oscar ceremonies and White House beanos, and entertains the troops overseas. Professional to his fingertips and prodigious in his energies, Bob Hope still appears on TV and has written several books.

with Dorothy Lamour in *My Favourite Brunette*

ESTHER WILLIAMS

E S T H E R   W I L L I A M S

Born Los Angeles, California, 8 August 1923

Swimming was glamorised and immortalised by 'Hollywood's Mermaid', as Esther Williams was widely known. From the mid-40s to the mid-50s, most of her films were smash hits – those that is, in which she swam. Onshore, she was never more than just passable, but there was never a more romantic sight than Esther taking to the water – gliding, twirling; backstroke, breaststroke; she dived, she somersaulted, she raced, she swam the channel; she rode trapezes and descended on water skis between jets of flame; she swam with Tom and Jerry. And all the time the gardenia in her hair remained intact, every hair remained in place, the warm eyes stayed clear, the strong white teeth gleamed, the make-up never slipped.

But if the effects were pure fantasy, the swimming was not. Remarkably, Esther Williams, although born near the heartland of movie country, never intended, or aspired to, movie stardom. By the time she was in her mid-teens, she had broken two world swimming records and was an almost certain candidate for the 1940 Olympics. However, while studying at LA City College she decided to join Billy Rose's 1939 Aquacade in San Francisco. She was spotted by an MGM scout but it took the studio the best part of a year to persuade the reluctant aquabat to sign a contract. It was Esther's good fortune that her figure was an asset to a bathing suit, and vice versa, and that she was very pretty –

especially in Technicolor. That she couldn't act, couldn't sing, couldn't dance didn't matter. She had an original gift to offer. Esther made a modest start as one of Mickey Rooney's amours in *Andy Hardy's Double Life* (1942), but was truly launched in *Bathing Beauty* (1944). She played a swimming instructor, the first of several, though sometimes the writers varied the formula to swimming star, including a real one, Annette Kellerman, in *Million Dollar Mermaid* (1952). Propped up by the staple stars of MGM's light-hearted romps of the period – Van Johnson, Red Skelton, Fernando Lamas – she kept cash registers ringing with films like *On An Island With You* (1948), *Neptune's Daughter* (1949) and *Pagan Love Song* (1950). In the mid-50s, after the flop of *Jupiter's Darling*, Esther departed MGM. In 1956 she made a serious attempt to go straight in *The Unguarded Moment* for Universal, but high dramatics really weren't her line and her film career foundered.

She maintained business interests in swimsuits and pools, and appeared internationally in live Swim Spectaculars. The 60s found her living in Spain where Fernando Lamas directed himself and her in a film which appears never to have been released, *The Magic Mountain*. In 1969 they married. Esther Williams' most quoted remark is 'All they ever did for me at MGM was to change my leading men and the water in the pool'.

in Million Dollar Mermaid

JOHN GARFIELD

JOHN GARFIELD

Real name **Julius Garfinkle**
Born **New York City, 4 March 1913**
Died **1952**

Director Elia Kazan, who unveiled Marlon Brando to the world, once called John Garfield 'the first of the natural off-the-street rebels'. Handsome in a dark, thickset, slightly coarse way, and with considerable charm and sensitivity simmering beneath the surface of his tough, street-wise personality, Garfield would undoubtedly have survived as a star far beyond the decade that made him famous. Alas, he fell victim to questioning by the House UnAmerican Activities Committee of the McCarthy era and refused to name friends. The encounter robbed him of work and probably precipitated the heart attack that killed him at 40.

The son of poor Jewish immigrants, Garfield grew up brawling on New York's Lower East Side and seemed destined for a delinquent life, but his intelligence won him a scholarship to the Ouspenskaya Drama School. He then had an apprenticeship with Eva Le Gallienne's repertory company before spending time as a cross-country vagrant. He fetched up as an extra in *Footlight Parade* (1933) for Warner Bros., then returned to New York, joined the Group theatre, and began to enjoy a Broadway career until Warner Bros. signed him to a seven-year contract where he made an immediate success in *Four Daughters* (1938). From then on he was almost always cast to type – gangsters, bums, slum boys with aspirations. The titles tell it all: *They Made Me A Criminal* (1939), *Dust Be My Destiny* (1939),

Dangerously They Live (1942), with occasional excursions into 'clean' roles which revealed his wider gifts (with Spencer Tracy in *Tortilla Flat* on loan to MGM in 1942; the ex-soldier adapting to blindness in *Pride Of The Marines*, 1945; a poor back-street violinist taken up in more ways than one by the rich and dipsomaniacal Joan Crawford in *Humoresque*, 1947). But his vehicles were largely sub-Bogart or Cagney stuff, and one of his most famous roles came along when he was again on loanout to MGM, who starred him opposite Lana Turner in James Cain's erotic murder thriller, *The Postman Always Rings Twice* (1946), in which they made an electric duo.

When his contract expired Garfield refused to renew, deciding instead to form his own company. The first fruit was the powerful boxing film, *Body And Soul* (1947), directed by Abraham Polonsky, and considered to be the star's best movie. He went to 20th Century-Fox to give an appealing portrayal as Gregory Peck's Jewish soldier friend in *Gentleman's Agreement* (1947), then again with Polonsky – whose own career would be badly damaged by McCarthy – and for his own company, made *Force Of Evil* (1948). Married with two children, he died just prior to taking the lead in a New York stage revival of Clifford Odets' 'Golden Boy' – ironically, the very play in which he had first gained attention in a supporting role.

with Ann Doran and Anne E. Todd in *Pride Of The Marines*

INGRID BERGMAN

INGRID BERGMAN

Born Stockholm, Sweden, 29 August 1915
Died 1982

When Ingrid Bergman died in 1982, aged 67, after a long struggle with cancer, she had won the true affection and respect of her colleagues and her public. It was a far cry from the rebuffs received when she left her doctor husband and her young daughter for Italian director Roberto Rossellini, by whom she bore an illegitimate child. They married in 1950, but against such a backlash of American moral indignation – she was even callled 'Hollywood's apostle of degradation' by one outraged US senator – that Ingrid was banned from US movies for some years. The marriage to Rossellini later produced twins, but did not last and, in 1958, she married Swedish producer Lars Schmidt. The outcry might have been less hysterical in the case of another actress, but Bergman had become a popular and powerful symbol of purity and integrity. Already an established star in her native Sweden, she came to Hollywood for David Selznick in 1939 to star in an American remake of her Swedish success, *Intermezzo*. From the outset she refused to slot into Hollywood's glamour machine, insisting on retaining the freshness of her natural Nordic prettiness that later flowered into womanly radiance.

In a working life that lasted almost four decades, Ingrid Bergman – who also enjoyed a successful stage career – made comparatively few films, but she has at least eight to her credit which have acquired lasting fame and popularity. After *Intermezzo* she was cast as the cockney barmaid terrorised by Spencer Tracy in *Dr Jekyll And Mr Hyde* (1941), overcoming the obvious drawback of her accent by the sheer conviction of her emotional expression. The following year guaranteed her immortality when she starred opposite Humphrey Bogart in *Casablanca*. There followed in swift succession *For Whom The Bell Tolls* (1943) with Gary Cooper, *Gaslight* (1944) for which she won her first Oscar, and Hitchcock's *Spellbound* in 1945, the year she also made *The Bells Of St Mary's* with Bing Crosby which brought her another nomination. This run reached its peak when she was magically paired with Cary Grant in another Hitchcock, the superb *Notorious* (1946).

After a couple of flops, including *Joan Of Arc* (1948), she took her fateful trip to Italy to make a film for Rossellini. None of her Italian films was successful but, in 1956, America forgave her and she was cast as the claimant to the Romanov throne, *Anastasia* (1956). Atonement extended to giving her another Oscar but she deserved it far more for her last film, *Autumn Sonata* (1977), which earned only a nomination. This was her first Swedish film for almost 40 years, and confirmed all that James Agee had noted in 1943: 'Miss Bergman not only bears a startling resemblance to an imaginable human; she really knows how to act, in a blend of poetic grace with quiet realism...'

with Paul Henreid and Claude Rains in *Casablanca*

L A N A   T U R N E R

L A N A   T U R N E R

Real name **Julia Jean Turner**
Born **Wallace, Idaho, 8 February 1921**

Lana Turner became a very big star in the 40s, and continued to flourish in the 50s in glossy Technicolor love stories, melodramas and weepies in which her perfect blonde coiffeur, discreet voluptuousness and endless array of fabulous clothes were often the most interesting items. She was, in fact, the last of the great studio-manufactured glamour queens, a breed which disappeared until Joan Collins triumphantly resurrected it recently in *Dynasty*.

As a teenager Lana was spotted by the editor of 'The Hollywood Reporter' while sipping soda in a drugstore (*not* Schwab's as legend has it), and sent to see director Mervyn LeRoy who gave her a tiny part in *They Won't Forget* (1937). Dubbed 'the sweater girl' (knitwear and Miss Turner's endowments were all but inseparable at the time), she served an apprenticeship in a number of forgotten films before MGM took her up and promoted her as a wartime pin-up and, soon, a major star. But Lana's permanent entourage of secretaries, hairdressers, make-up men, and other minders signally failed to protect her from herself. She acquired seven husbands – including bandleader Artie Shaw and erstwhile Tarzan, Lex Barker – broke her heart over Tyrone Power who didn't marry her, and became disastrously involved with Johnny Stompanato, a Mafia-connected gangster. To be fair, Miss Turner did not know the truth for some time. She was rescued from his clutches when her daughter, Cheryl Crane, fatally stabbed him. Cheryl was acquitted on grounds of justifiable homicide, and Lana's career was, if anything, enhanced by the ensuing scandalous revelations.

Never a great actress, she had first made a real impression in *Ziegfeld Girl* (1941). Over the years, she developed a definite and elegant screen presence and a deft way with melodrama and, although she received her only Oscar nomination for *Peyton Place* (1957), it was her steamy affair with John Garfield in *The Postman Always Rings Twice* (1946) that remains her most famous achievement. In the wake of the Stompanato scandal, she shone in Douglas Sirk's lavish remake of *Intimation Of Life* (1959), as an actress who neglects her daughter for her career. The 60s and 70s saw a gradual phasing out of her career, and she ventured into stage work and a little TV.

Miss Turner's eventful private life, and her varied career, are in themselves a perfect cameo of this period in Hollywood history. She has told all, with a startling ingenuousness that repays study, in a recent autobiography entitled 'Lana: The Lady, The Legend, The Truth', in which she treats the reader to an extraordinary display of frankness in recounting the strains of being a Love Goddess and, in her own estimation, a legend. When the initial shock has worn off, you can't help liking her.

with John Garfield in *The Postman Always Rings Twice*

GEORGE SANDERS

GEORGE SANDERS

Born St Petersburg, Russia, 3 July 1906
Died 1972

'Dear World, I am leaving you because I am bored.' Thus read the suicide note of the urbane George Sanders, who took an overdose of sleeping pills in a Spanish hotel room to end a career in which he was prominent in well over 100 films, many of them ranging from merely forgettable to very poor, and in which he was almost always the redeeming feature. Everything about Sanders stamped him as unusual in the canon of movie stars during Hollywood's Golden Age. British to the bone, with a distinctive, silky, and not a little acidulous, speaking voice, he was born in Russia where his family lived. When the Revolution struck, they returned to England, where George was educated at Brighton and Manchester, training for the textile business in which he then went to work. Bored with that, he embarked on a business in South America concerning the sale of tobacco, but it was a failure. He returned to London and, with no particular ambition to be an actor, appears to have gone into the theatre for want of something better to do. He made a few British films in the 30s before being contracted by 20th Century-Fox for whom he made his Hollywood debut in *Lloyds Of London* (1936).

He was typecast as a smooth villain very quickly, and brought a unique air of distinction to every possible variety of cad, criminal and manipulator for the rest of his days, although there were one of two excursions into romantic drama (*Rage In Heaven*, 1941, opposite Ingrid Bergman) and, after the war, a couple of classy period pieces, most notably *The Picture Of Dorian Gray* (1945), in which he excelled as Lord Henry Wootton, the first of his long line of weary cynics. In the late 30s and early 40s he played *The Saint* and *The Falcon* four times each but, during the war, he specialised in a succession of Nazis and other related hate figures of the period. Suave, handsome, witty and intelligent both on and off the screen, the high point of Sanders' career was his portrayal of Addison de Witt, the cruelly cynical theatre critic in *All About Eve* (1950), a performance still relished today, and for which he won a well-deserved Oscar in this gem of a film which starred Bette Davis in *her* finest role. The landmark of his career prior to *All About Eve* was the lead in *The Moon And Sixpence* (1942) where, as the Gauguin figure, Charles Strickland, he was able to portray a new form of caddery. After his Oscar, however, it was downhill all the way. He never stopped working, always received major billing, but rarely made a movie which had much to recommend it.

In private life, Sanders married four times. Apart from being one of the glamorous Zsa Zsa Gabor's seemingly limitless number of husbands, he also (later) married her sister, Magda. In 1960, he published an autobiography, aptly titled *Memoirs Of A Professional Cad*.

in The Saint in London

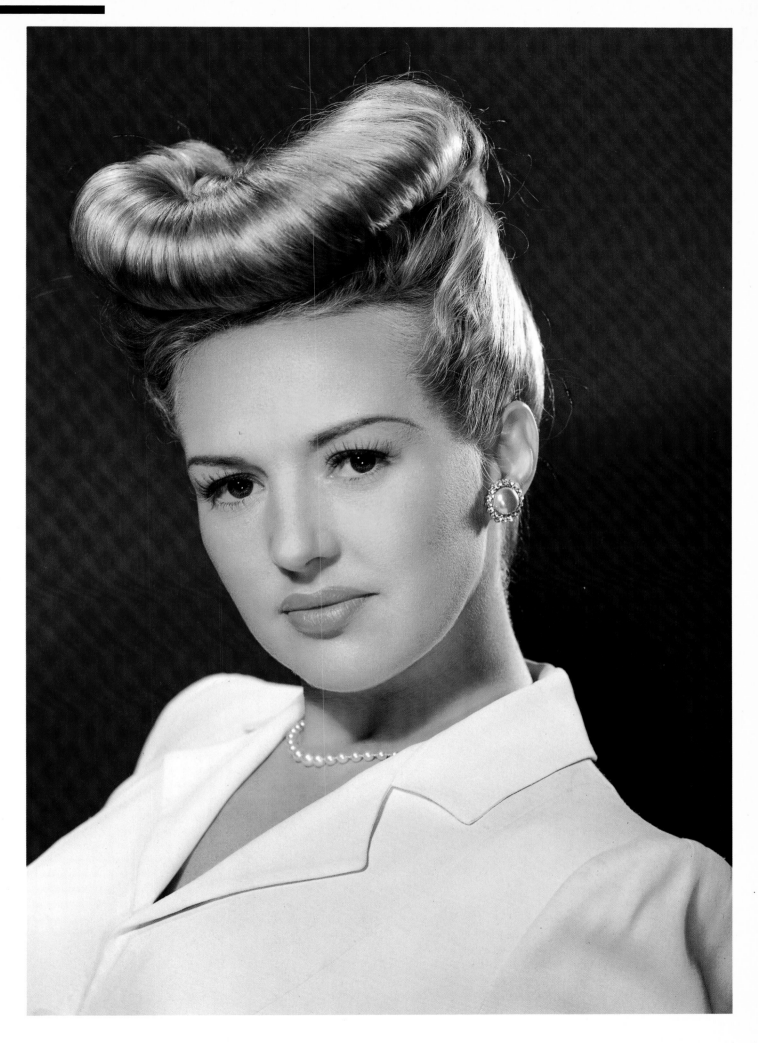

BETTY GRABLE

BETTY GRABLE

Real name **Ruth Elizabeth Grable**
Born **St Louis, Missouri, 18 December 1916**
Died **1973**

One of Betty Grable's last, and best, films was *How To Marry A Millionaire* (1953) with Lauren Bacall and Marilyn Monroe, after which, it is reported, Betty said to Marilyn, 'Honey, I've had it. Go get yours. It's your turn now'. And, indeed, Marilyn inherited Betty's mantle as surely as Betty herself had displaced Alice Faye in the 40s.

The Fox musicals were brash and colourful extravaganzas, trademarked by a succession of leading ladies collectively known as the Fox Blondes. There was no blonder, nor more popular Fox girl than Betty Grable, although it took her a long time to get there. Trained as a dancer she made her debut at 14 in the chorus line of an early musical called *Let's Go Places* (1930) before becoming a Goldwyn Girl. When Goldwyn dropped her, she was shunted between several studios for several years, playing featured roles, but nobody seemed to know how to groom her for the stardom they sensed possible. In 1937 she married former child star Jackie Coogan and was taken up by Paramount. Both experiences where short-lived and Grable left Hollywood to play the second lead in 'Du Barry Was A Lady' on Broadway. This gained her the attention that had hitherto passed her by, and 20th Century-Fox signed her to replace an ill Alice Faye, opposite Don Ameche in *Down Argentine Way* (1940). Throughout the war and post-war years she starred in a plethora of formula musicals, barely distinguishable from each other. These included *Coney Island* (1943), *Sweet Rosie O'Grady* (1944), *The Dolly Sisters* (1946), and four with Dan Dailey including *Mother Wore Tights* (1947), so titled to stem the tide of protest after she had failed to show her legs – insured with Lloyds for a million dollars – in *The Shocking Miss Pilgrim* earlier that year. Those much vaunted legs, Grable's absolute ordinariness, and her good cheer somehow touched a chord in the 40s which made her the American forces' number one pin-up and elevated her to being one of the biggest box-office attractions of the decade. Yet she gave the following honest assessment of herself: 'As a dancer I couldn't outdance Ginger Rogers or Eleanor Powell. As a singer I'm no rival to Doris Day. As an actress I don't take myself seriously. I had a little bit of looks without being in the big beauty league. Maybe I had sincerity. And warmth . . . I don't think I've ever had a good review. My films didn't get them either . . .'

With the decline of her popularity in the 50s, Betty returned to theatre work, including a stint on Broadway in 'Hello Dolly'. Her 20-year marriage to bandleader Harry James ended in 1965 and she herself died of lung cancer eight years later aged 56. It was an undistinguished career really, but she left behind a wealth of happy memories for an entire generation.

with Robert Young in *Sweet Rosie O'Grady*